MAKING

YOUR OWN

GOURMET

CHOCOLATE

DRINKS

MAKING YOUR OWN GOURMET CHOCOLATE DRINKS

Hot Drinks,
Cold Drinks,
Sodas, Floats,
Shakes,
and More!

Mathew
Tekulsky

Illustrations by
Clair Moritz-Magnesio

Crown Publishers, Inc.
New York

Published by Crown Publishers, Inc.
201 East 50th Street, New York, New York 10022.
Member of the Crown Publishing Group.

Random House, Inc. New York, Toronto, London, Sydney, Auckland
http://www.randomhouse.com/

CROWN is a trademark of Crown Publishers, Inc.

Printed in the United States of America

Design by Nancy Kenmore

Library of Congress Cataloging-in-Publication Data
Tekulsky, Mathew.
Making your own gourmet chocolate drinks: hot drinks, cold drinks,
sodas, floats, shakes, and more! / Mathew Tekulsky;
illustrations by Clair Moritz-Magnesio.–1st ed.
Includes index.
1. Chocolate.   2. Beverages.   I. Title.
TX817.C4T45   1996
641.8'75–dc20   95-30346

ISBN: 0-517-70265-7

10   9   8   7   6   5   4

To my mother,
Patience Fish Tekulsky,
who first introduced me
to the joys of chocolate!

Acknowledgments

I would like to thank the great team of designer Nancy Kenmore, illustrator Clair Moritz-Magnesio, and production editor Kim Hertlein, for making my cookbooks look so great. Thanks as well to Gail Shanks, for setting up author appearances. Thanks, as always, to Michelle Sidrane and Ann Patty, for their continued support. And thanks as always to my literary agent, Jane Jordan Browne, and to my editor, Brandt Aymar. Special thanks to all of the wonderful people I have met at my book signings and who purchase my books. You are the greatest!

Contents

MAKING YOUR OWN GOURMET CHOCOLATE DRINKS

Introduction

Ever since the Aztec emperor Montezuma introduced the Spanish explorer Hernán Cortés to the wonders of a chocolate beverage called xocolatl (meaning "bitter water") in 1519, the proliferation of chocolate, first as a beverage, then as a food, has continued throughout the world. • After the Spanish sweetened the drink with sugar, it became a favorite at court, appealing greatly to the nobles of the time. • Eventually, the use of this beverage spread throughout Europe, and in the mid-seventeenth century, a conglomeration of chocolate houses in London played a primary role in the business and social activities of the day. • It was not until the middle of the next century that chocolate arrived in Colonial America, although it was still consumed as a beverage even at this late date. • And while the invention of the milk chocolate bar did not occur until 1876, the popularity of chocolate as a beverage–both hot and cold–continues to this day. • With this book, you will be able to make a great combination of drinks using the fabulous cocoa bean, just as Montezuma did.

Whether you choose to mix your chocolate with fruit such as raspberries, blueberries, or cherries; nuts such as hazelnuts, almonds, or peanuts; candies made from maple sugar, mint, or licorice; or liqueurs such as Grand Marnier, amaretto, or Kahlúa, you will be sure to experience a wide assortment of delectable tastes–yet all with one thing in common: They are all made with chocolate! • We will include hot drinks for cold winter days, as well as cold drinks for the blazing days of summer–and many drinks that you can enjoy on all the days in between. • So settle back and get your taste buds ready. • After all, chocolate is not called "Food of the Gods" for nothing. • Enjoy!

The Various
Types of Chocolate
You Can Use

All chocolate is derived from the cocoa bean, which is the seed of the cocoa tree, *Theobroma cacao* (Theobroma means food of the gods).

The cocoa tree grows in tropical climates, between twenty degrees north and twenty degrees south of the equator.

Although the cocoa tree is native to Mexico and Central and South America, more than half of the world's cocoa beans today are produced in the western African countries of the Ivory Coast, Ghana, Nigeria, and Cameroon. The remaining cocoa beans are largely produced in Brazil, Indonesia, and Malaysia, and to a lesser extent in other countries such as Ecuador, the Dominican Republic, Mexico, Colombia, Papua New Guinea, and Venezuela.

The cocoa tree produces pods throughout the year, in which seeds (or beans) are contained. After the pods are cut from the tree, they are split open and the beans are removed.

After fermenting for a few days, the beans are dried in the sun for a few more days, and are then packed for shipment to chocolate factories around the world.

When the cocoa beans arrive at the chocolate factory, they are roasted, after which the shells are removed to reveal the cocoa nibs–the "meat" of the bean.

The cocoa nibs are then ground to create a pasty liquid known as chocolate liquor–which consists of cocoa solids as well as cocoa butter. This is unsweetened baking chocolate, which is poured into molds and cooled before being packaged as bars.

In order to create semisweet (or bittersweet) baking chocolate, sugar (and often additional cocoa butter) is added to the chocolate liquor; and in order to create milk chocolate, sugar, additional cocoa butter, and milk are added to the chocolate liquor. Semisweet chocolate and milk chocolate are also poured into molds and cooled before being packaged as bars.

In order to create unsweetened cocoa powder, the chocolate liquor is sent through a hydraulic press that extracts most of the cocoa butter and leaves a "press cake" consisting primarily of the cocoa solids. This press cake is then finely ground and sifted, thus creating the unsweetened cocoa powder.

Dutch-processed cocoa powder is produced by treating the chocolate liquor with an alkali. This gives the resulting cocoa powder a milder, less acidic taste, as well as a darker brown color than ordinary unsweetened cocoa powder.

White chocolate is not really chocolate at all, since it is composed only of cocoa butter, sugar, milk solids, and flavorings such as vanilla–and has no cocoa solids in it.

Chocolate syrup consists of unsweetened cocoa powder, sugar, and water.

Sweetened chocolate powder consists of unsweetened cocoa powder and sugar.

Storing Your Chocolate

No matter which type of chocolate you use, it is important to store it in the proper manner in order to make sure that it lasts as long as possible and stays as fresh as possible before you use it.

In general, unsweetened, semisweet, white, and milk chocolate should be stored in a cool, dry place (about 60° F. to 70° F.). Chocolate should not be stored in the refrigerator, as the cold temperature caused by refrigeration can cause a gray or white film (or "bloom") to appear on the surface of the chocolate as the cocoa butter rises to the surface. This bloom can occur if the chocolate is exposed to too much heat as well; however, the bloom will disappear when you melt the chocolate, and it has no effect on the taste of the chocolate.

If chocolate is exposed to too much moisture (such as from refrigeration), the moisture can cause the sugar crystals in the chocolate to rise to the surface of the chocolate, thus causing a gray or white "sugar bloom." This bloom also disappears when the chocolate is melted, and has no effect on the taste of the chocolate.

Unsweetened cocoa powder and sweetened chocolate powder should be stored in an airtight container in a cool, dry place (about 60° F. to 70° F.). They should not be stored in the refrigerator, as the moisture from refrigeration can cause the powder to become lumpy.

Chocolate syrup should be stored in the refrigerator after it is opened.

When stored properly, unsweetened baking chocolate should remain fresh for about 2 years; semisweet baking chocolate for about 1½ years; white and milk chocolate for about 1 year; unsweetened cocoa powder and sweetened chocolate powder for about 2 years; and chocolate syrup for about 1 year.

Using Your Chocolate

Because different types of chocolate have varying amounts of sugar and cocoa butter in them, they can be used in conjunction with certain ingredients in order to achieve a desired result.

For instance, drinks that are made with unsweetened baking chocolate or unsweetened cocoa powder can be sweetened by adding maple syrup, eggnog, or liqueurs such as crème de cacao.

Meanwhile, drinks that are made with semisweet chocolate or chocolate syrup can incorporate ingredients such as cinnamon, espresso, and malted milk powder without having to add any extra sugar.

And unsweetened cocoa powder, which is low-fat, can be used with yogurt and nonfat milk to create a delicious low-cal drink.

How you decide to use your chocolate is largely a matter of personal preference, so feel free to use your imagination to create the chocolate drinks that you like best.

Making Chocolate
Whipped Cream

You may wish to top some of the drinks in this book with chocolate-flavored whipped cream.

Here is how you make it: Place ¼ cup heavy cream in a bowl and add 1 teaspoon chocolate syrup (or 1 teaspoon unsweetened cocoa powder and ½ teaspoon regular granulated sugar) to the heavy cream. Whip up the cream along with the chocolate (or cocoa and sugar), and use this chocolate-flavored whipped cream to top off some of your favorite gourmet chocolate drinks.

A Note on Ingredients

1. With chocolate baking bars, 1 ounce is a measurement of weight, not volume.

2. I use chocolate syrup, but an equal amount of sweetened chocolate powder can be used as well.

3. I use white chocolate chips, but you can also use the equivalent amount of a white chocolate baking bar or white chocolate candy, depending on your taste.

4. When using unsweetened cocoa powder to make hot cocoa, it is best to first make a paste with the cocoa powder and a small amount of milk or whatever liquid you are using; then stir this paste into the rest of the liquid over low heat. This will allow the cocoa powder to dissolve into the liquid in the smoothest fashion possible, without causing lumps of cocoa powder to occur in the liquid.

5. I use regular granulated sugar.

6. Unless otherwise specified, I use whole milk, but low-fat or even nonfat milk can also be used, depending on your taste.

7. I use low-fat yogurt, but nonfat yogurt can also be used.

8. It is always best to use fresh whipped cream—generally about ¼ cup per drink.

9. Feel free to use packaged or fresh coconut milk (if available); and feel free to substitute fresh chopped coconut for sweetened shredded coconut (as a garnish).

10. I use sliced marshmallows, but miniature marshmallows can also be used.

11. Unless otherwise specified, all nuts are raw and shelled.

12. If you wish to make more (or fewer) servings of these drinks, simply multiply (or divide) the amount of each ingredient to provide for the number of servings that you wish to make.

Hot *Gourmet* Chocolate *Drinks*

Hot Chocolate Royale

The half-and-half makes this drink much richer than a standard hot chocolate. (For a standard hot chocolate, simply use regular milk instead of the half-and-half.)

$\frac{1}{2}$ ounce semisweet baking
    chocolate
1 cup half-and-half

$\frac{1}{4}$ cup heavy cream,
    whipped
Sweetened chocolate
    powder

Stir the chocolate into the half-and-half in a saucepan over low heat for 3 to 4 minutes, or until hot (do not boil). Pour into a mug and top with the whipped cream and chocolate powder.

Serves 1

Hot Cocoa

In all of its variations, this drink is a traditional favorite that is sure to warm you up on a cold winter day.

2 teaspoons unsweetened
   cocoa powder
2 teaspoons sugar
2 cups milk
   Whipped cream
   (optional)

Sweetened chocolate
   powder or unsweetened
   cocoa powder (optional)

Stir the cocoa powder and the sugar into 4 teaspoons of the milk in a saucepan, until a smooth paste is formed. Pour the rest of the milk into the saucepan and stir the mixture constantly over low heat for 5 to 6 minutes, or until it is hot (do not boil). Pour into 2 mugs and top with whipped cream and sprinkle with chocolate powder or cocoa powder, if desired.

Serves 2

Variations: For a Vanilla Hot Cocoa, stir ⅛ teaspoon vanilla extract into each drink before topping with whipped cream and sprinkling with chocolate powder or cocoa powder, if desired.

For a Mint Hot Cocoa, stir ⅛ teaspoon mint extract into each drink before topping with whipped cream and sprinkling with chocolate powder or cocoa powder, if desired.

For an Orange Hot Cocoa, stir ⅛ teaspoon orange extract into each drink before topping with whipped cream and sprinkling with chocolate powder or cocoa powder, if desired.

Dark-White Hot Chocolate

The white chocolate chips add their own distinctive taste to the traditional taste of the semisweet chocolate.

½ ounce semisweet baking chocolate
1 tablespoon white chocolate chips
2 cups milk
½ cup heavy cream, whipped

Sweetened chocolate powder or additional white chocolate chips, for garnish

Stir the semisweet chocolate and 1 tablespoon white chocolate chips into the milk in a saucepan over low heat for 5 to 6 minutes, or until hot (do not boil). Pour into 2 mugs, top with the whipped cream, and garnish with chocolate powder or white chocolate chips.

Serves 2

Butterscotch Hot Chocolate

The taste of this drink goes back and forth between choco-late and butterscotch–what could be better?

1 tablespoon chocolate
   syrup
1 tablespoon butterscotch
   topping
1 cup milk

Whipped cream
(optional)
Sweetened chocolate
powder or ground
nutmeg, for garnish
(optional)

Stir the chocolate syrup and the butterscotch topping into the milk in a saucepan over low heat for 3 to 4 minutes, or until hot (do not boil). Pour the mixture into a mug and top with whipped cream and chocolate powder or nutmeg, if desired.

Serves 1

Honey Hot Chocolate

The honey adds a special taste to the hot chocolate.

$^{1}/_{2}$ ounce unsweetened
  baking chocolate
1 tablespoon honey
$^{1}/_{8}$ teaspoon ground
  cinnamon

1 cup milk
$^{1}/_{4}$ cup heavy cream,
  whipped

Stir the chocolate, honey, and cinnamon into the milk in a saucepan over low heat for 3 to 4 minutes, or until hot (do not boil). Pour into a mug and top with whipped cream.

Serves 1

Maple Hot Chocolate

This drink will make you think of autumn in New England.

$^{1}/_{2}$ ounce unsweetened
  baking chocolate
2 tablespoons maple syrup
1 cup milk

$^{1}/_{4}$ cup heavy cream,
  whipped
Maple sugar candy, for
  garnish (optional)

Stir the chocolate and the maple syrup into the milk in a saucepan over low heat for 3 to 4 minutes, or until hot (do not boil). Pour into a mug, top with whipped cream, and garnish with small pieces of maple sugar candy, if desired.

Serves 1

Mint Hot Chocolate

You may wish to substitute Chocolate Whipped Cream (page 20) for the regular whipped cream in this drink, in which case the chocolate powder would be optional. Please feel free to substitute Chocolate Whipped Cream for the regular whipped cream in the variation as well. It is up to you.

1 tablespoon chocolate
  syrup
1 cup milk
$\frac{1}{8}$ teaspoon mint extract
$\frac{1}{4}$ cup heavy cream,
  whipped

Sweetened chocolate
powder
Fresh mint sprig, for
garnish

Stir the chocolate syrup into the milk in a saucepan over low heat for 3 to 4 minutes, or until hot (do not boil). Pour this mixture into a mug and stir in the mint extract. Top with whipped cream and chocolate powder and garnish with a fresh mint sprig.

Serves 1

Variation: For an Orange Hot Chocolate, substitute $\frac{1}{8}$ teaspoon orange extract for the mint extract and proceed as directed above. Top with whipped cream and sprinkle with grated orange peel.

Cinnamon Hot Chocolate

The great taste of cinnamon adds a nice accent to the hot chocolate.

1 tablespoon chocolate
  syrup
⅛ teaspoon ground
  cinnamon
1 cup milk
¼ cup heavy cream,
  whipped

Additional ground
  cinnamon
Cinnamon stick, for
  garnish (optional)

Stir the chocolate syrup and ⅛ teaspoon cinnamon into the milk in a saucepan over low heat for 3 to 4 minutes, or until hot (do not boil). Pour into a mug, top with whipped cream, sprinkle with cinnamon, and garnish with a cinnamon stick, if desired.

Serves 1

Spiced Hot Chocolate

Spices and chocolate taste great together–whether you use the vanilla or the almond extract.

2 tablespoons chocolate
   syrup
¼ teaspoon ground
   cinnamon
⅛ teaspoon ground allspice
⅛ teaspoon ground nutmeg

¼ teaspoon vanilla extract
2 cups milk
½ cup heavy cream,
   whipped
   Sweetened chocolate
   powder

Stir the chocolate syrup, spices, and vanilla extract into the milk in a saucepan over low heat for 5 to 6 minutes, or until hot (do not boil). Pour into 2 mugs, top with whipped cream, and sprinkle with chocolate powder.

Serves 2

Variation: Substitute ¼ teaspoon almond extract for the vanilla extract. Proceed as directed above.

Espresso Hot Chocolate

Whether you use the espresso or the coffee in this drink, it is sure to satisfy!

1 tablespoon chocolate
   syrup
1½ ounces freshly brewed
   espresso, still piping hot
1 cup milk

¼ cup heavy cream,
   whipped
Sweetened chocolate
   powder or ground
   cinnamon

Stir the chocolate syrup and the espresso into the milk in a saucepan over low heat for 3 to 4 minutes, or until hot (do not boil). Pour into a mug, top with whipped cream, and sprinkle with chocolate powder or cinnamon.

Serves 1

Variation: For a Coffee Hot Chocolate, substitute ¼ cup freshly brewed coffee for the espresso and use ¾ cup milk. Proceed as directed above.

Hot Cocoa-Espresso Eggnog

This drink is like a chocolate eggnog latte–great for the holidays!

1 teaspoon unsweetened
    cocoa powder
¾ cup eggnog
¼ cup milk

1½ ounces freshly brewed
    espresso, still piping hot
¼ cup heavy cream,
    whipped
Ground nutmeg

Stir the cocoa powder into 2 teaspoons of the eggnog in a saucepan, until a smooth paste is formed. Pour the rest of the eggnog along with the milk and the espresso into the saucepan and stir the mixture constantly over low heat for 3 to 4 minutes, or until hot (do not boil). Pour into a mug and top with whipped cream and nutmeg.

Serves 1

Variation: For a richer drink, substitute ¼ cup half-and-half for the milk. Proceed as directed above.

Tea Hot Chocolate

The subtle taste of the tea comes through in this delicious drink.

> 1 tablespoon chocolate
>   syrup
> ⅔ cup milk
> ⅓ cup freshly brewed
>   English Breakfast or
>   another black tea, still
>   piping hot

> ⅛ teaspoon vanilla extract
>   (optional)
> ¼ cup heavy cream,
>   whipped
>   Sweetened chocolate
>   powder

Stir the chocolate syrup into the milk in a saucepan over low heat for 3 to 4 minutes, or until hot (do not boil). Add the tea and stir so that all of the ingredients are mixed together. Pour this mixture into a mug, add the vanilla extract, if desired, and top with whipped cream and chocolate powder.

Serves 1

Coconut Hot Chocolate

The great taste of coconut and chocolate mix beautifully in this drink.

2 cups milk
½ cup sweetened shredded coconut

1 ounce unsweetened baking chocolate

Preheat the oven to 350° F. Place 1 cup of the milk and the coconut in a saucepan and stir occasionally over low heat for 3 to 4 minutes, or until hot (do not boil). Strain the milk into a container and place the coconut on a baking sheet. Bake the coconut in the oven until it turns brown, about 8 to 10 minutes. Meanwhile, stir the coconut-flavored milk and the chocolate into the remaining milk in a saucepan over low heat for 3 to 4 minutes, or until hot (do not boil). Pour this mixture into 2 mugs and top with the browned coconut.

Serves 2

Malted Hot Chocolate

Add the taste of malted milk to your hot chocolate with this drink.

½ ounce semisweet baking chocolate	Whipped cream (optional)
1 tablespoon malted milk powder	Malted milk powder, for garnish (optional)
1 cup milk	

Stir the chocolate and 1 tablespoon malted milk powder into the milk in a saucepan over low heat for 3 to 4 minutes, or until hot (do not boil). Pour into a mug and top with the whipped cream and sprinkle with malted milk powder, if desired.

Serves 1

Chocolate Mint Candy
Hot Chocolate

Enjoy eating the candy as you drink this drink!

1 piece of chocolate mint candy	1 cup milk
½ ounce semisweet baking chocolate	¼ cup heavy cream, whipped

Place the candy at the bottom of a mug. Stir the chocolate into the milk in a saucepan over low heat for 3 to 4 minutes, or until hot (do not boil). Pour over the candy in the mug and top with whipped cream.

Serves 1

Variation: For an English Toffee Hot Chocolate, substitute 1 piece of English toffee candy for the chocolate mint candy. Proceed as directed above.

Raisin Hot Chocolate

The great taste of the raisins mixes well with the taste of the chocolate–whether white or dark. (Feel free to use 1 tablespoon fresh sliced apricot–peeled or unpeeled–instead of the raisins in this drink.)

> 1 tablespoon raisins
> $\frac{1}{2}$ ounce semisweet baking
>   chocolate
>
> 1 cup milk
> $\frac{1}{4}$ cup heavy cream,
>   whipped

Place the raisins at the bottom of a mug. Stir the chocolate into the milk in a saucepan over low heat for 3 to 4 minutes, or until hot (do not boil). Pour over the raisins in the mug and top with whipped cream.

Serves 1

Variation: For a Raisin–White Hot Chocolate, substitute 1 tablespoon white chocolate chips for the semisweet chocolate and proceed as directed above.

Pecan Hot Chocolate

The pecans and macadamia nuts float in this drink, so you can enjoy spooning them off the surface of the hot chocolate!

1 tablespoon pecans
½ ounce semisweet baking
  chocolate
1 cup milk

¼ cup heavy cream,
  whipped
Ground pecans, for
  garnish

Place 1 tablespoon pecans at the bottom of a mug. Stir the chocolate into the milk in a saucepan over low heat for 3 to 4 minutes, or until hot (do not boil). Pour over the pecans in the mug and top with whipped cream and ground pecans.

Serves 1

Variation: For a Macadamia Nut Hot Chocolate, substitute 1 tablespoon macadamia nuts for the pecans and proceed as directed above. Garnish with ground macadamia nuts.

Ice Cream Hot Cocoa

The ice cream melts into the hot cocoa and provides a sweetener as well.

1 teaspoon unsweetened
  cocoa powder
1 cup milk

1 scoop chocolate, vanilla,
  or coffee ice cream

Stir the cocoa powder into 2 teaspoons of the milk in a saucepan, until a smooth paste is formed. Pour the rest of the milk into the saucepan and stir the mixture constantly over low heat for 3 to 4 minutes, or until it is hot (do not boil). Pour into a mug and add the ice cream.

Serves 1

Cold
Gourmet
Chocolate
Drinks

Coffee Chocolate Milk

This is a great drink for the summer!

1 cup milk
1 tablespoon chocolate
syrup
1 cup brewed coffee,
chilled

Ice cubes
Ground cinnamon
(optional)

Mix the milk, chocolate syrup, and coffee together and pour over ice in 2 tall glasses. Sprinkle with cinnamon, if desired.

Serves 2

Chocolate Soda Float

The ice cream melts into the soda and adds its own distinct flavor to this drink–delicious!

$^3/_4$ cup chocolate soda,
chilled
1 scoop chocolate, vanilla,
or coffee ice cream

Whipped cream
(optional)
Sweetened chocolate
powder (optional)

Pour the chocolate soda into a tall glass. Add the ice cream and top with whipped cream and chocolate powder, if desired.

Serves 1

Chocolate Milk Float

This drink turns a glass of chocolate milk into a special treat.

1 teaspoon chocolate
  syrup
1 cup milk
1 scoop chocolate ice
  cream

$^{1}/_{4}$ cup heavy cream,
  whipped
Sweetened chocolate
  powder

Stir the chocolate syrup into the milk in a tall glass. Add the ice cream and top with whipped cream and chocolate powder.

Serves 1

Variation: For a Vanilla–Chocolate Milk Float, substitute 1 scoop vanilla ice cream for the chocolate ice cream and use 1 tablespoon chocolate syrup instead of 1 teaspoon chocolate syrup. Proceed as directed above.

Chocolate Egg Cream

If you stir the chocolate syrup up from the bottom of the glass slowly and carefully (being sure to stop at just the right time!), you can create three layers of color in this drink—dark brown at the bottom, light brown in the middle, and white at the top.

¼ cup milk
¾ cup carbonated water, chilled

2 tablespoons chocolate syrup

Pour the milk into a tall glass. Add the carbonated water and chocolate syrup and stir briskly until a head of foam is created.

Serves 1

Variations: For a richer drink, substitute ¼ cup half-and-half or heavy cream for the milk and proceed as directed above.

For a Chocolate Phosphate, omit the milk and use 1 cup carbonated water instead of ¾ cup carbonated water. Proceed as directed above.

Chocolate-Strawberry
Ice Cream Soda

Treat yourself to bites of the strawberry ice cream as you drink this drink.

4 tablespoons chocolate
   syrup
2 cups milk
1 cup carbonated water

2 scoops strawberry ice
   cream
Fresh strawberries, for
   garnish

Stir 2 tablespoons of the chocolate syrup into 1 cup of the milk in each of 2 tall glasses. Add ½ cup carbonated water and 1 scoop ice cream to each glass and garnish with fresh strawberries.

Serves 2

Ginger-Chocolate Float

Chocolate ice cream can be mixed with four different sodas—each with a different effect.

¾ cup ginger ale, chilled
1 scoop chocolate ice cream

Whipped cream (optional)
Sweetened chocolate powder (optional)

Pour the ginger ale into a tall glass. Add the ice cream and top with whipped cream and chocolate powder, if desired.

Serves 1

Variations: For a Root Beer—Chocolate Float, substitute ¾ cup chilled root beer for the ginger ale and proceed as directed above.

For a Cream Soda—Chocolate Float, substitute ¾ cup chilled cream soda for the ginger ale and proceed as directed above.

For a Cherry-Chocolate Float, substitute ¾ cup chilled cherry soda for the ginger ale and proceed as directed above.

Chocolate-Marshmallow Blend

Chocolate and marshmallows–what a combination! There's nothing like it!

1 cup milk
1 tablespoon chocolate
   syrup
2 tablespoons sliced
   marshmallows
   Ice cubes
¼ cup heavy cream,
   whipped

Sweetened chocolate
   powder
Additional sliced
   marshmallows, for
   garnish

Mix the milk, chocolate syrup, and 2 tablespoons marshmallows in a blender for 10 to 15 seconds, or until smooth. Pour over ice in a tall glass, top with whipped cream and chocolate powder, and garnish with marshmallows.

Serves 1

Chocolate-Eggnog Blend

This drink will remind you of the winter holidays on a warm summer evening.

½ cup eggnog
½ cup milk
1 teaspoon unsweetened
   cocoa powder

Ice cubes
Ground nutmeg

Mix the eggnog, milk, and cocoa powder in a blender for 15 to 20 seconds, or until smooth. Pour over ice in a tall glass and sprinkle with nutmeg.

Serves 1

Variation: For a Banana-Chocolate-Eggnog Blend, add 1 peeled and sliced banana to the eggnog, milk, and cocoa powder. Proceed as directed above.

Chocolate-Banana Blend

Serve this drink immediately, before it has time to settle.

1 cup milk
1 banana, peeled and
  sliced
1 teaspoon unsweetened
  cocoa powder

¼ cup heavy cream,
  whipped
Additional banana
  slices, for garnish

Mix the milk, banana, and cocoa powder in a blender for 15 to 20 seconds, or until smooth. Pour into a tall glass, top with whipped cream, and garnish with slices of banana.

Serves 1

Chocolate-Mango Blend

Please feel free to use other fruit with this drink, such as strawberries, raspberries, blueberries, or peach slices.

$\frac{1}{2}$ *cup mango, sliced*
$\frac{1}{2}$ *cup milk*

1 tablespoon chocolate
syrup

Mix all the ingredients in a blender for 15 to 20 seconds, or until smooth.

Serves 1

Variation: For a Chocolate-Pineapple Blend, substitute $\frac{1}{2}$ cup pineapple, peeled and sliced, for the mango.

Chocolate-Orange Yogurt Blend

Drink this one right away, while it is still frothy.

$\frac{1}{4}$ *cup plain yogurt, low-fat*
$\frac{1}{4}$ *cup milk, nonfat*
$\frac{1}{2}$ *cup orange juice*

1 teaspoon chocolate
syrup

Mix all the ingredients in a blender for 10 to 15 seconds, or until smooth.

Serves 1

Chocolate-Raspberry
Yogurt Blend

Use this low-fat elixir as a pick-me-up between meals—or anytime else.

½ cup raspberry yogurt, low-fat
½ cup milk, nonfat

1 tablespoon unsweetened cocoa powder

Mix all the ingredients in a blender for 10 to 15 seconds, or until smooth.

Serves 1

Variations: For a Chocolate–Peach Yogurt Blend, substitute ½ cup peach yogurt for the raspberry yogurt. Proceed as directed above.

For a Chocolate–Strawberry Yogurt Blend, substitute ½ cup strawberry yogurt for the raspberry yogurt. Proceed as directed above.

For a Chocolate–Blueberry Yogurt Blend, substitute ½ cup blueberry yogurt for the raspberry yogurt. Proceed as directed above.

Chocolate-Espresso Yogurt Blend

This low-fat drink tastes great–a chocolate-espresso delight!

½ cup plain yogurt, low-fat
½ cup milk, nonfat
1½ ounces brewed espresso, chilled

2 tablespoons chocolate syrup
1 teaspoon sugar

Mix all the ingredients in a blender for 10 to 15 seconds, or until smooth.

Serves 1

Chocolate-Coffee Shake

Two of our favorite flavors blend together perfectly in this drink.

1 scoop chocolate ice cream
1 scoop coffee ice cream
1 cup milk

Whipped cream (optional)
Sweetened chocolate powder (optional)

Mix the ice creams and the milk in a blender for 15 to 20 seconds, or until smooth. Pour into a tall glass and top with whipped cream and chocolate powder, if desired.

Serves 1

Chocolate-Raspberry Shake

Whether you use raspberries, strawberries, or kiwifruit to flavor this drink, it is sure to pack a fruity "punch." For a low-cal version, substitute chocolate frozen yogurt for the chocolate ice cream.

1 scoop chocolate ice cream
¼ cup fresh raspberries
½ cup milk

¼ cup heavy cream, whipped
Additional raspberries, for garnish

Mix the ice cream, ¼ cup raspberries, and milk in a blender for 15 to 20 seconds, or until smooth. Pour into a tall glass, top with whipped cream, and garnish with fresh raspberries.

Serves 1

Variations: For a Chocolate-Strawberry Shake, substitute ¼ cup fresh strawberries for the raspberries and proceed as directed above. Garnish with fresh strawberries.

For a Chocolate-Kiwi Shake, substitute ¼ cup peeled and sliced fresh kiwifruit for the raspberries and proceed as directed above. Garnish with peeled and sliced fresh kiwifruit.

Chocolate-Pistachio Shake

The great tastes of chocolate and pistachio mix well in this drink.

1 cup milk
2 scoops pistachio ice cream
1 teaspoon unsweetened cocoa powder

Whipped cream (optional)
Ground pistachio nuts, raw or roasted, unsalted, for garnish (optional)

Mix the milk, ice cream, and cocoa powder in a blender for 15 to 20 seconds, or until smooth. Pour into a tall glass and top with whipped cream and sprinkle with ground pistachio nuts, if desired.

Serves 1

White Chocolate-Vanilla Shake

This beautiful white drink is like a vanilla milkshake with the flavor of white chocolate in it. Drink it right away while it is still frothy.

2 tablespoons white chocolate chips

1½ cups milk
2 scoops vanilla ice cream

Stir the chocolate chips into the milk in a saucepan over low heat for 5 to 6 minutes, or until hot (do not boil). Chill in the refrigerator and mix with the ice cream in a blender for 15 to 20 seconds, or until smooth.

Serves 2

Variation: For a White Chocolate–Chocolate Shake, substitute chocolate ice cream for the vanilla ice cream. Proceed as directed above.

Vanilla-Chocolate-Orange Shake

The vanilla, chocolate, and orange flavors mix beautifully in this drink. Feel free to substitute 1 cup chocolate ice cream for the vanilla ice cream and cocoa powder.

> 1 cup vanilla ice cream
> ½ cup orange juice
>
> 1 teaspoon unsweetened
> cocoa powder

Mix all the ingredients in a blender for 15 to 20 seconds, or until smooth.

Serves 1

Variations: For a Vanilla-Chocolate-Tangerine Shake, substitute ½ cup tangerine juice for the orange juice. Proceed as directed above.

For a Vanilla-Chocolate-Lemon Shake, substitute 1 tablespoon lemon juice for the orange juice. Proceed as directed above.

Chocolate-Pineapple-Coconut Shake

Pineapple and coconut add a tropical accent to this chocolate shake!

2 scoops chocolate ice cream
¼ cup coconut milk
¼ cup pineapple juice
½ cup milk

Whipped cream (optional)
Sweetened shredded coconut or pineapple slices, for garnish (optional)

Mix the ice cream, coconut milk, pineapple juice, and milk in a blender for 15 to 20 seconds, or until smooth. Pour into 2 tall glasses and top with whipped cream and garnish with sweetened shredded coconut or slices of pineapple, if desired.

Serves 2

Chocolate-Lemon Sherbet Shake

This low-cal shake is a great refresher for a hot summer afternoon!

1 cup lemon sherbet
½ cup milk, nonfat

1 teaspoon unsweetened
cocoa powder

Mix all the ingredients in a blender for 15 to 20 seconds, or until smooth.

Serves 1

Variations: For a Chocolate–Lime Sherbet Shake, substitute 1 cup lime sherbet for the lemon sherbet and proceed as directed above.

For a Chocolate–Orange Sherbet Shake, substitute 1 cup orange sherbet for the lemon sherbet and proceed as directed above.

Chocolate Malted Shake

Please feel free to substitute 2 scoops of vanilla ice cream and 1 tablespoon unsweetened cocoa powder for the chocolate ice cream in this drink—which is a classic!

2 scoops chocolate ice cream	Whipped cream (optional)
1 cup milk	Sweetened chocolate powder (optional)
1 tablespoon malted milk powder	

Mix the ice cream, milk, and malted milk powder in a blender for 15 to 20 seconds, or until smooth. Pour into a tall glass and top with whipped cream and chocolate powder, if desired.

Serves 1

Variations: For a Banana-Chocolate Malted Shake, add ½ peeled and sliced banana to the ice cream, milk, and malted milk powder. Proceed as directed above. Garnish with peeled and sliced banana, if desired.

For a Banana-Strawberry-Chocolate Malted Shake, add ¼ peeled and sliced banana and 4 strawberries to the ice cream, milk, and malted milk powder. Proceed as directed above. Garnish with peeled and sliced banana and/or a fresh strawberry, if desired.

Vanilla-Mint-Chocolate Malted Shake

Enjoy this minty-malty refresher while you are sitting by the pool in the summer.

1 cup milk

2 scoops vanilla ice cream

1/8 teaspoon mint extract

1 tablespoon unsweetened cocoa powder

1 teaspoon malted milk powder

Whipped cream (optional)

Sweetened chocolate powder (optional)

Mix the milk, ice cream, mint extract, cocoa powder, and malted milk powder in a blender for 15 to 20 seconds, or until smooth. Pour into a tall glass and top with whipped cream and chocolate powder, if desired.

Serves 1

Chocolate Chip Cookie Shake

If you blend this drink for a shorter time, you will have larger pieces of chocolate chip cookie in it.

1 cup milk	Whipped cream
2 scoops chocolate ice	(optional)
cream	Additional chocolate
4 chocolate chip cookies	chip cookie, for garnish
	(optional)

Mix the milk, ice cream, and 4 cookies in a blender for 10 to 15 seconds, or until smooth. Pour into a tall glass and top with whipped cream and garnish with a chocolate chip cookie, if desired.

Serves 1

Chocolate-Peanut Butter Shake

Chocolate and peanut butter is a classic combination—enjoy!

2 scoops chocolate ice
  cream
½ cup milk
1 tablespoon peanut
  butter, creamy

Unsalted, roasted
peanuts, for garnish
(optional)

Mix the ice cream, milk, and peanut butter in a blender for 15 to 20 seconds, or until smooth. Pour into a tall glass and garnish with peanuts, if desired.

Serves 1

Variation: For a Vanilla-Chocolate—Peanut Butter Shake, substitute 2 scoops of vanilla ice cream and 1 teaspoon unsweetened cocoa powder for the chocolate ice cream. Proceed as directed above.

Gourmet *Chocolate* Drinks *with* Liquor

Hot *Gourmet* Chocolate *Drinks* with *Liquor*

Crème de Cacao Hot Chocolate

Chocolate! Chocolate! Chocolate! From the top to the bottom!

$\frac{1}{2}$ ounce unsweetened
   baking chocolate
1 cup milk
2 tablespoons crème de
   cacao

$\frac{1}{4}$ cup heavy cream,
   whipped
Sweetened chocolate
   powder

Stir the chocolate into the milk in a saucepan over low heat for 3 to 4 minutes, or until hot (do not boil). Pour into a mug, add the crème de cacao, and top with whipped cream and chocolate powder.

Serves 1

Rum Hot Chocolate

Whether you use the rum or the brandy, this drink is sure to satisfy!

$\frac{1}{2}$ *ounce semisweet baking*
  chocolate
1 *cup milk*
2 *tablespoons rum*

$\frac{1}{4}$ *cup heavy cream,*
  whipped
Ground nutmeg

Stir the chocolate into the milk in a saucepan over low heat for 3 to 4 minutes, or until hot (do not boil). Pour into a mug, add the rum, and top with whipped cream and nutmeg.

Serves 1

Variation: For a Brandy Hot Chocolate, substitute 2 tablespoons brandy for the rum and proceed as directed above.

Grand Marnier Hot Chocolate

The Grand Marnier bursts into your mouth along with the chocolate in this very tasty drink, and the orange peel on top adds just the right touch.

1 tablespoon chocolate
   syrup
1 cup milk
2 tablespoons Grand
   Marnier liqueur

$\frac{1}{4}$ cup heavy cream,
   whipped
Grated orange peel, for
   garnish

Stir the chocolate syrup into the milk in a saucepan over low heat for 3 to 4 minutes, or until hot (do not boil). Pour into a mug, add the Grand Marnier, top with whipped cream, and sprinkle with grated orange peel.

Serves 1

Variation: For an Amaretto Hot Chocolate, substitute 2 tablespoons of amaretto liqueur for the Grand Marnier and substitute ground almonds for the grated orange peel. Proceed as directed above.

Anisette Hot Chocolate

This one is a great after-dinner drink—like a dessert in itself!

½ ounce semisweet baking
  chocolate

1 cup milk

2 tablespoons anisette
  liqueur

¼ cup heavy cream,
  whipped

1 piece red or black
  licorice, for garnish
  (optional)

Stir the chocolate into the milk in a saucepan over low heat for 3 to 4 minutes, or until hot (do not boil). Pour into a mug, add the anisette, top with whipped cream, and garnish with a piece of licorice, if desired.

Serves 1

Whiskey Hot Cocoa

Warm your spirits–along with your insides–with this whiskey-flavored hot cocoa drink!

1 teaspoon unsweetened
    cocoa powder
1 teaspoon sugar
1 cup milk
$\frac{1}{8}$ teaspoon ground
    cinnamon

1 tablespoon whiskey
$\frac{1}{4}$ cup heavy cream,
    whipped
    Additional ground
    cinnamon

Stir the cocoa powder and sugar into 2 teaspoons of the milk in a saucepan, until a smooth paste is formed. Add the rest of the milk and $\frac{1}{8}$ teaspoon cinnamon and stir the mixture constantly over low heat for 3 to 4 minutes, or until it is hot (do not boil). Pour into a mug, add the whiskey, and top with whipped cream and cinnamon.

Serves 1

Chartreuse Hot Chocolate

The Chartreuse and the pistachio nuts complement each other nicely in this drink.

*½ ounce semisweet baking
    chocolate*
1 cup milk
*1 tablespoon green
    Chartreuse liqueur*

*¼ cup heavy cream,
    whipped*
*Ground pistachio nuts,
    raw or roasted,
    unsalted, for garnish*

Stir the chocolate into the milk in a saucepan over low heat for 3 to 4 minutes, or until hot (do not boil). Pour into a mug, add the Chartreuse, and top with the whipped cream and pistachio nuts.

Serves 1

Chambord Hot Chocolate

The taste of the raspberry liqueur is enhanced by the fresh raspberries in this drink.

*½ ounce semisweet baking
    chocolate
1 cup milk
1 tablespoon Chambord
    liqueur*

*¼ cup heavy cream,
    whipped
Fresh raspberries, for
garnish*

Stir the chocolate into the milk in a saucepan over low heat for 3 to 4 minutes, or until hot (do not boil). Pour into a mug, add the Chambord, top with whipped cream, and garnish with fresh raspberries.

Serves 1

Variation: For a Chambord—White Hot Chocolate, substitute 1 tablespoon white chocolate chips for the semisweet chocolate and proceed as directed above.

Amaretto-Kahlúa
Hot Chocolate

This almond-coffee hot chocolate provides a great combination of tastes.

$\frac{1}{2}$ ounce semisweet baking
chocolate

1 cup milk

1 tablespoon amaretto
liqueur

1 tablespoon Kahlúa
liqueur

$\frac{1}{4}$ cup heavy cream,
whipped

Ground cinnamon or
sweetened chocolate
powder

Stir the chocolate into the milk in a saucepan over low heat for 3 to 4 minutes, or until hot (do not boil). Pour into a mug, add the amaretto and Kahlúa, top with whipped cream, and sprinkle with cinnamon or chocolate powder.

Serves 1

Variation: For a Brandy-Kahlúa Hot Chocolate, substitute 1 tablespoon brandy for the amaretto and proceed as directed above.

Brandy-Grand Marnier
Hot Chocolate

The brandy adds a nice accent to the orange flavor of the
Grand Marnier in this drink.

$\frac{1}{2}$ *ounce semisweet baking*
  chocolate
1 *cup milk*
1 *tablespoon brandy*
1 *tablespoon Grand*
  Marnier liqueur

$\frac{1}{4}$ *cup heavy cream,*
  whipped
Grated orange peel, for
  garnish

Stir the chocolate into the milk in a saucepan for 3 to 4 minutes, or until hot (do not boil). Pour into a mug, add the
brandy and Grand Marnier, and top with whipped cream
and grated orange peel.

Serves 1

Bailey's-Frangelico Hot Chocolate

The distinctive taste of the Bailey's mixes well with the Frangelico in this drink—and it tastes great with the amaretto too!

$\frac{1}{2}$ ounce unsweetened
  baking chocolate
1 cup milk
2 tablespoons Bailey's
  Original Irish Cream
  liqueur

1 tablespoon Frangelico
  liqueur
$\frac{1}{4}$ cup heavy cream,
  whipped
Sweetened chocolate
  powder

Stir the chocolate into the milk in a saucepan over low heat for 3 to 4 minutes, or until hot (do not boil). Pour into a mug, add the Bailey's and Frangelico, and top with whipped cream and chocolate powder.

Serves 1

Variation: For a Bailey's-Amaretto Hot Chocolate, substitute 1 tablespoon amaretto liqueur for the Frangelico and proceed as directed above.

Whiskey-Coconut Hot Chocolate

Bring the taste of the tropics to your palate with this marvelous drink!

*½ ounce unsweetened
baking chocolate*
*2 tablespoons coconut
milk*
1 teaspoon sugar
1 cup milk

1 tablespoon whiskey
*¼ cup heavy cream,
whipped*
*Sweetened shredded
coconut, for garnish*

Stir the chocolate, coconut milk, and sugar into the milk in a saucepan over low heat for 3 to 4 minutes, or until hot (do not boil). Pour into a mug, add the whiskey, and top with whipped cream and sweetened shredded coconut.

Serves 1

Grand Marnier-Frangelico Hot Cocoa

The orange, hazelnut, and chocolate flavors, when sipped through whipped cream, are a real delight!

1 teaspoon unsweetened cocoa powder

1 cup milk

1 tablespoon Grand Marnier liqueur

1 tablespoon Frangelico liqueur

¼ cup heavy cream, whipped

Grated orange peel or ground hazelnuts, for garnish

Stir the cocoa powder into 2 teaspoons of the milk in a saucepan, until a smooth paste is formed. Add the rest of the milk and stir the mixture constantly over low heat for 3 to 4 minutes, or until it is hot (do not boil). Pour into a mug, add the Grand Marnier and Frangelico, and top with whipped cream and orange peel or hazelnuts.

Serves 1

Variation: For a Grand Marnier–Crème de Menthe Hot Cocoa, substitute 1 tablespoon crème de menthe for the Frangelico and proceed as directed above. Garnish with grated orange peel or a fresh mint sprig.

Crème de Menthe-Kahlúa Hot Cocoa

The mint provides a nice accent for the Kahlúa in this drink.

1 teaspoon unsweetened
   cocoa powder
1 cup milk
1 tablespoon crème de
   menthe

1 tablespoon Kahlúa
   liqueur
$\frac{1}{4}$ cup heavy cream,
   whipped
Fresh mint sprig, for
   garnish

Stir the cocoa powder into 2 teaspoons of the milk in a saucepan, until a smooth paste is formed. Pour the rest of the milk into the saucepan and stir the mixture constantly over low heat for 3 to 4 minutes, or until it is hot (do not boil). Pour into a mug, add the crème de menthe and Kahlúa, top with whipped cream, and garnish with a fresh mint sprig.

Serves 1

Frangelico-White
Hot Chocolate

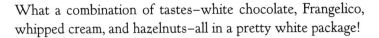

What a combination of tastes—white chocolate, Frangelico, whipped cream, and hazelnuts—all in a pretty white package!

1 tablespoon white
  chocolate chips
1 cup milk
2 tablespoons Frangelico
  liqueur

¼ cup heavy cream,
  whipped
Ground hazelnuts, for
  garnish

Stir the chocolate chips into the milk in a saucepan over low heat for 3 to 4 minutes, or until hot (do not boil). Pour into a mug, add the Frangelico, and top with whipped cream and ground hazelnuts.

Serves 1

Whiskey-Rum-White Hot Chocolate

This white drink will warm you up on a cold winter night, in front of a fire.

1 tablespoon white
  chocolate chips
1 cup milk
1 tablespoon whiskey

1 tablespoon rum
¼ cup heavy cream,
  whipped

Stir the chocolate chips into the milk in a saucepan over low heat for 3 to 4 minutes, or until hot (do not boil). Pour into a mug, add the whiskey and rum, and top with whipped cream.

Serves 1

Crème de Cacao-Brandy-Kahlúa Hot Cocoa

The crème de cacao, brandy, and Kahlúa mix together in this drink to create a very special taste.

1 teaspoon unsweetened cocoa powder	1 tablespoon Kahlúa liqueur
1 cup milk	1/4 cup heavy cream, whipped
1 teaspoon crème de cacao	Sweetened chocolate powder
1 teaspoon brandy	

Stir the cocoa powder into 2 teaspoons of the milk in a saucepan, until a smooth paste is formed. Pour the rest of the milk into the saucepan and stir the mixture constantly over low heat for 3 to 4 minutes, or until it is hot (do not boil). Pour into a mug, add the crème de cacao, brandy, and Kahlúa, and top with whipped cream and chocolate powder.

Serves 1

Brandy-Rum-Coffee
Hot Chocolate

The coffee-chocolate mixture combined with the brandy and rum makes a great assortment of tastes.

*½ ounce semisweet baking
  chocolate
½ cup milk
½ cup freshly brewed
  coffee, still piping hot
1 tablespoon brandy*

*1 tablespoon rum
¼ cup heavy cream,
  whipped
Sweetened chocolate
powder*

Stir the chocolate into the milk and coffee in a saucepan over low heat for 3 to 4 minutes, or until hot (do not boil). Pour into a mug, add the brandy and rum, and top with whipped cream and chocolate powder.

Serves 1

Crème de Cacao-Amaretto Hot Cocoa Eggnog

The crème de cacao and amaretto add a unique accent to this eggnog mixture.

1 *teaspoon unsweetened cocoa powder*	1 *teaspoon amaretto liqueur*
½ *cup eggnog*	¼ *cup heavy cream, whipped*
½ *cup milk*	
1 *teaspoon crème de cacao*	*Ground nutmeg*

Stir the cocoa powder into 2 teaspoons of the eggnog in a saucepan, until a smooth paste is formed. Pour the rest of the eggnog along with the milk into the saucepan and stir the mixture constantly over low heat for 3 to 4 minutes, or until hot (do not boil). Pour into a mug, add the crème de cacao and amaretto, and top with whipped cream and nutmeg.

Serves 1

Variation: For a Rum Hot Cocoa Eggnog, substitute 1 teaspoon rum for the crème de cacao and the amaretto. Proceed as directed above.

Cold *Gourmet* Chocolate
Drinks with *Liquor*

Crème de Cacao-Frangelico Delight

This white drink features the taste of chocolate from the crème de cacao, along with a hazelnut accent from the Frangelico–scrumptious!

2 tablespoons crème de
  cacao
1 tablespoon Frangelico
  liqueur
1 cup milk
Ice cubes

¼ cup heavy cream,
  whipped
Sweetened chocolate
  powder or ground
  hazelnuts, for garnish

Stir the crème de cacao and Frangelico into the milk and pour over ice in a tall glass. Top with whipped cream and chocolate powder or hazelnuts.

Serves 1

Variations: For a Crème de Cacao–Rum Delight, substitute 1 tablespoon rum for the Frangelico and proceed as directed above. Garnish with sweetened chocolate powder.

For a Crème de Cacao–Grand Marnier Delight, substitute 1 tablespoon Grand Marnier liqueur for the Frangelico and proceed as directed above. Garnish with sweetened chocolate powder or grated orange peel.

Tea-Frangelico Chocolate Delight

The Frangelico provides a hazelnut aftertaste in this drink–a great refresher!

1/3 cup brewed English Breakfast or another black tea, chilled

1 tablespoon chocolate syrup

1 teaspoon Frangelico liqueur

2/3 cup milk

Ice cubes

Whipped cream (optional)

Sweetened chocolate powder (optional)

Stir the tea, chocolate syrup, and Frangelico into the milk and pour over ice in a tall glass. Top with whipped cream and chocolate powder, if desired.

Serves 1

Chocolate-Mint Ice Cream Float

The chocolate and mint liqueurs make a refreshing contribution to this drink—and the chocolate ice cream gives you an extra "punch" as well.

1 tablespoon crème de cacao

1 tablespoon crème de menthe

³⁄₄ cup milk
Ice cubes

1 scoop chocolate ice cream

¹⁄₄ cup heavy cream, whipped

Sweetened chocolate powder

Fresh mint sprig, for garnish

Stir the crème de cacao and the crème de menthe into the milk and pour over ice in a tall glass. Add the ice cream, top with whipped cream, sprinkle with chocolate powder, and garnish with a fresh mint sprig.

Serves 1

Crème de Cacao Soda

The crème de cacao gives your cola an extra "zing," along with the great taste of chocolate.

¾ cup cola	¼ cup heavy cream,
¼ cup carbonated water	whipped
Ice cubes	Sweetened chocolate
2 tablespoons crème de	powder
cacao	

Pour the cola and carbonated water over ice in a tall glass. Add the crème de cacao and top with whipped cream and chocolate powder.

Serves 1

Crème de Cacao-Raspberry Yogurt Blend

The crème de cacao sweetens this drink and gives it its chocolate taste.

½ cup plain yogurt, low-fat
½ cup milk, nonfat
½ cup fresh raspberries

2 tablespoons crème de cacao

Mix all the ingredients in a blender for 15 to 20 seconds, or until smooth.

Serves 1

Variations: For a Crème de Cacao–Blueberry Yogurt Blend, substitute ½ cup fresh blueberries for the raspberries and proceed as directed above.

For a Crème de Cacao–Strawberry Yogurt Blend, substitute ½ cup fresh strawberries for the raspberries and proceed as directed above.

Chocolate-Kirsch Yogurt Blend

The subtle taste of the kirsch (and the framboise) comes through in this low-cal pick-me-up.

½ cup cherry yogurt, low-fat

½ cup milk, nonfat

1 teaspoon unsweetened cocoa powder

1 tablespoon kirsch liqueur

Mix all the ingredients in a blender for 10 to 15 seconds, or until smooth.

Serves 1

Variation: For a Chocolate–Framboise Yogurt Blend, substitute ½ cup raspberry yogurt for the cherry yogurt and substitute 1 tablespoon framboise liqueur for the kirsch liqueur. Proceed as directed above.

Crème de Cacao-Banana Crush

Enjoy this slushy, banana-tasting treat on a hot day!

1 scoop chocolate ice
  cream
½ cup milk
1 tablespoon crème de
  cacao
1 tablespoon banana
  liqueur

¼ cup crushed ice
  Whipped cream
  (optional)
  Banana, peeled and
  sliced, for garnish
  (optional)

Mix the ice cream, milk, crème de cacao, banana liqueur, and crushed ice in a blender for 15 to 20 seconds, or until smooth. Pour into a tall glass and top with whipped cream and banana slices, if desired.

Serves 1

Rum-Chocolate Shake

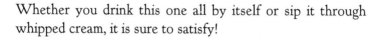

Whether you drink this one all by itself or sip it through whipped cream, it is sure to satisfy!

½ cup milk

1 scoop chocolate ice cream

2 tablespoons rum

Whipped cream (optional)

Sweetened chocolate powder (optional)

Mix all the ingredients in a blender for 10 to 15 seconds, or until smooth. Pour into a tall glass and top with whipped cream and chocolate powder, if desired.

Serves 1

Chocolate-Crème de Menthe Shake

The crème de menthe adds a delightful, minty accent to this chocolate shake.

> 1 scoop chocolate ice
>   cream
> ½ cup milk
> 1 tablespoon crème de
>   menthe

> Ice cubes
> ¼ cup heavy cream,
>   whipped
> Fresh mint sprig, for
>   garnish

Mix the ice cream, milk, and crème de menthe in a blender for 15 to 20 seconds, or until smooth. Pour over ice, top with whipped cream, and garnish with a fresh mint sprig.

Serves 1

Strawberry-Amaretto Chocolate Shake

The strawberry-almond taste of this drink combines well with the chocolate taste of the cocoa powder–delightful!

½ cup milk
1 scoop vanilla ice cream
¼ cup fresh strawberries
1 teaspoon unsweetened cocoa powder
1 tablespoon amaretto liqueur

Whipped cream (optional)
Additional fresh strawberries or sliced almonds, for garnish (optional)

Mix the milk, ice cream, ¼ cup strawberries, cocoa powder, and amaretto in a blender for 15 to 20 seconds, or until smooth. Pour into a tall glass and top with whipped cream and garnish with fresh strawberries or sliced almonds, if desired.

Serves 1

Index